Click Ti

Getting Your Digital Photo Just Right

Cynthia L. Baron and Daniel Peck

Table of Contents

Click This!
Getting Your Digital Photo Just Right
Cynthia L. Baron and Daniel Peck

Peachpit Press
1249 Eighth Street
Berkeley, CA 94710
510/524-2178 • 800/283-9444
510/524-2221 (fax)

Find us on the World Wide Web at: www.peachpit.com

To report errors, please send a note to errata@Peachpit.com

Peachpit Press is a division of Pearson Education

ISBN 0-321-12530-4

9 8 7 6 5 4 3 2 1

Printed and bound in the United States of America

Introducing Digital Photography

Photography is experiencing a revolution. Sales of digital cameras are quickly over-taking those of film-based cameras, and bringing with them a new way of work-ing with pictures.

Digital cameras are a decade old, but they used to be so expensive and complex that only technology-savvy pro-fessionals used them. But, just as the Brownie camera made photography affordable to almost anyone at the beginning of the 20th century, recent advances have brought the price of digital cameras down to as low as $100.

This affordability unlocks a door to options we've always wanted and could only dream of before. A digital camera offers truly instant images. You can shoot a picture and look at it immediately. In less than five minutes, you can trans-fer that picture to a computer. Moments later, you can print it, post it on a Web page or email it to friend. You never have to buy film or visit the drugstore to have it processed. And the camera is just as easy to use as your as your trusty Kodak Instamatic. Maybe easier.

Advantages of Digital Photography

Why should you take the plunge and go digital? What's so different about digital photography?

- **Instant Gratification**. Most digital cameras have a built-in screen, so right away, you can see the picture you just took. You will never again wonder if a shot came out right.

- **Reusability**. Digital cameras use storage cards to save pictures. After you transfer your work to a computer, you can delete the shots from the card and start over. No more film!

- **Usability**. Because you can transfer your pictures to your computer directly from the camera, you can take a picture, transfer it to the computer and send it to a friend in a matter of minutes. And you can use the digital image in many ways. From a single image, you can save a high quality version for printing and make a lower resolution copy for a Web page or email.

○ **Duplication**. A film camera produces a picture as either a negative for print-making or a positive for use as a slide. If the original is lost or damaged, so is the picture. A digital image can be copied many times and not lose quality. And like all computer data, it can be backed up. No more boxes full of unmarked negatives taking up closet space.

○ **Size**. A film camera has to be big enough to hold a roll of film, so even the smallest aren't that small. Digital cameras can be made smaller (Figure 1.1) and in different shapes, including cameras with swivel lenses, so you can take a picture of a subject that is not directly in front of the camera.

Figure 1.1 Dan loves his Nikon FM, but he can fit the Olympus 510 digicam in his shirt pocket.

Digital Photos and Your Computer

A faster computer will be a better editing tool, and one you'll enjoy using more. Most digital cameras ship with image-editing software. Before you purchase a digital camera, check the software's requirements.

Although software is nearly always included with digital cameras, you don't have to use it. Many cameras can plug into a USB connector on your computer and transfer pictures without adding any software to your computer.

RAM

The more memory (RAM) your computer has, the more easily you can work with your digital photographs. 128 MB is the minimum we recommend. For any serious retouching or other editing of your photos, 256 MB is better. Your RAM needs depend on what type of editing you want to do and how you plan on using your photos, but in general, you can never have too much memory.

Storage

Depending on the resolution you used when you shot the picture, a single digital photograph can take up anywhere from a few kilobytes for a low quality, Web-only photo to a couple of megabytes of space on your hard drive for a nice 4″ × 6″ color print. As you add more pictures, they will quickly fill up even a good-sized hard drive. Image editing software may also demand a fair amount of free space on the hard drive.

If your computer doesn't have at least one gigabyte of free hard-drive space, you might want to consider upgrading it, or adding a second drive. Some computers allow you to easily add external hard drives. If this is not an option, removable storage devices like Zip drives can take the strain off your system. And if your computer came with a CD-R (a recordable CD drive), you can put images on CDs to help manage your files.

CD Recorders

Computers made in the last couple of years often have built-in CD recorders, often referred to as "burners." There are two kinds of burners:

o **CD-RW**. These are rewriteable, which means that you can erase and reuse the same CD-RW disk over and over.

o **CD-R**. These can only write onto a CD one time. Once an area of the CD-R media is used, it can't be erased and used again, even if you use a CD-RW disk.

Although CD-RW burners are more flexible, either type will work just fine for storing your photos.

You can store up to 675 MB of image data on a single CD at the cost of less than a dollar. That ranges between 550 and 800 4″ × 6″ prints, depending on the picture quality you set on your camera. Remember that burning photos to a CD will not just save you hard drive space. It gives you a great medium to send photos to friends, relatives, and even customers (Figure 1.2).

 CD burners and plain old CD players look a lot alike but they are not the same thing. Although a CD burner can also play CDs, a CD player can't make a new CD. Check your owner's manual if you're not sure whether you have a burner or a player.

Figure 1.2 A CD recorder provides easy permanent storage for your digital masterpieces.

USB

USB is the most commonly used method of transferring pictures from a digital camera to a computer. You can plug many cameras into your computer's USB port (Figure 1.3) and transfer the photos directly onto the hard drive or other storage devices. If you're using your USB ports for other things (like a Palm device), a USB hub will allow you to attach multiple devices to the same port.

If you only have a standard serial port and can't add USB, you can buy an inexpensive adapter for USB compatibility. It takes a long time to transfer photos over a serial port with an adapter, so if this is your only option, you might want to consider using a card reader, instead of connecting the camera directly to your computer (see Chapter 4 for more information on these options).

Figure 1.3 USB ports are usually in the back of your computer with all the other ports and connectors.

 If your computer is running Windows 95, Windows NT, or a Macintosh system version 8.5 or earlier, you will have to upgrade the OS, since none of these support USB.

Buy Your Camera

Your first step when you get into digital photography is buying your camera. You'll inevitably find yourself navigating a vast landscape of jargon: *Megapixels, digital zoom, US warranty, accessories not included*. It's enough to make you want to remain safely in the film world. This chapter will help you learn the language and understand what you need to get started.

Resolution and Megapixels

The *resolution* of a digital camera, or the amount of detail that the camera records, is expressed in *megapixels*, which is a measurement of the number of sensors the camera uses to record the picture. The more megapixels, the better the picture and the more things you can do with it. But the importance of a camera's resolution depends on the kind of pictures you want. If you use a picture on a Web page or to make a small print, you won't see much difference between a top-of-the-line camera and a basic consumer model. If, on the other hand, you make a large print, the difference will be all too obvious (Figure 2.1.)

Figure 2.1 This picture looks pretty good at its original size. When enlarged, the lack of detail in the original begins to show.

- **1 Megapixel.** Although there are still 1-megapixel cameras available, they aren't usually a good choice. A 2-megapixel camera, for just a bit more, will yield noticeably better pictures.

- **2 Megapixels.** For most purposes, 2-megapixel cameras are the best balance between price and quality. You'll be able to make prints up to 5″ × 7″ with good results.

- **3 Megapixels.** With 3 megapixels, you can make prints as large as 8″ × 10″. If you demand a lot of your camera, you should consider one in this range.

○ **4+ Megapixels.** At 4 megapixels and beyond, you approach the professional realm. The extra features will be obvious only when you want to enlarge a small area of a photo, or to make an oversized print.

 Some cameras advertise an "effective" megapixel count. This means that they are using the electronics of the camera to imitate the effect of more pixels. This does not work very well. Always use the actual pixel count when comparing models.

Price Comparison Shopping

The first question to answer when shopping for anything is "What do you want to spend?" Digital cameras are available for as little as $100 and as much as several thousand.

○ **Basic (under $500).** For making snapshots, such as family photos and vacation pictures, this is likely to be your price range. The resolution of cameras in this range will be 2–3 megapixels. You will get quality pictures suitable for posting to a Web page or emailing to relatives, and prints of up to 4" × 6".

○ **Deluxe ($500–$800).** If you are used to the control that a traditional 35mm film camera gives you, like manual exposure and focus control, this should be your price range. You will get at least 4 megapixels of resolution, so enlargements up to 8″ × 10″ will still look good.

o **Professional (over $800).** At this price, camera resolution will be 5 megapixels or higher. Features include remote control, continuous shooting, and a broader array of auto and manual settings. Also in this range are the 35mm digital cameras with interchangeable lenses and a wide variety of accessories.

 Once you've decided on your price range, your shopping choices boil down to online/mail order or retail store. Retail stores will usually offer better support and service. Mail order/online merchants offer better prices, but won't help much with questions or problems. When you buy online or mail order, always pay by credit card. If there is a problem with your order, you will have more options.

Optical vs. Digital Zoom

A camera's zoom lets you make the subject appear closer without actually moving closer. When you do this by adjusting the lens it is known as *optical* zoom. When it is done by the camera's electronic circuitry, it is known as *digital* zoom. In simple terms, optical zoom is good, digital zoom, not so good.

Optical zoom is better because it records the image at full resolution, so you get a sharp image at any zoom level. Digital zoom, on the other hand, creates the effect of zooming by enlarging a portion of the image, just like you could do on your computer. But this results in a lower-resolution image (Figure 2.2).

Some inexpensive cameras don't have optical zoom. As this is very limiting, you should really consider models with 2 or 3× optical zoom.

Figure 2.2 At maximum optical zoom, the skyline is clear and sharp (left). Although digital zoom brings the skyline closer (right), the details are less sharp.

Comparing Battery Types

Most cameras support only one type of battery. Batteries are a major factor in a camera's portability and upkeep cost, so you should consider this feature carefully before you buy.

o **Lithium.** These batteries have the longest life between charges, and last a long time. The ones that recharge in the camera are handiest. Lithium batteries are harder to find than AA, and are considerably more expensive (usually $30 and up).

o **Alkaline.** These are the most common and least expensive type of standard batteries. However, they are not rechargeable.

o **NiCad (nickel cadmium).** Although they are more expensive than alkalines, they can be recharged. The disadvantage of NiCads is that they do not last as long between charges as alkalines do before needing replacement. NiCads can only be recharged 50 times or so.

o **NiMH (nickel metal hydride).** The best of both worlds. They last as long as alkalines, but are rechargeable. The drawback is price—they cost as much as $3 per battery and require a special type of charger. Since they can be recharged hundreds of times, they are a worthwhile investment.

Don't toss NiMh, lithium and NiCad batteries in the trash when their life is over. The heavy metals they contain contaminate the environment. Check with your local waste authority for disposal tips.

Some cameras can use an external battery pack that plugs in where the AC adaptor goes and will power the camera for many hours. But since they are an extra item outside the camera, they are not always convenient to use.

Adapters

Cameras that use rechargeable lithium batteries include an AC adapter. To recharge the batteries, you either remove the battery, place it in the adapter, then plug it into an outlet, or plug the camera directly into an outlet with the AC adapter. Either way, recharging takes a few hours.

Cameras that use AA batteries will likely need a separate AC adapter. You probably won't be able to use the camera as a recharger. Most cameras will operate without batteries if plugged into an AC outlet (with an adapter), but some models may require a different adapter than the one that recharges the batteries.

Comparing Storage Media

There are three types of storage cards in today's market: SmartMedia, Compact Flash, and Memory Sticks. Capacities range from 4 to 256 megabytes. Most cameras include an 8 or 16 MB card. You may want to buy extra, larger capacity cards. Prices for all three types range from $20–$50.

o **SmartMedia.** These cards are wafer thin, and about two inches square. Their main disadvantage is that the contacts are exposed. If they get dirty, the camera may not be able to read the card. Rubbing the exposed area with a pencil eraser will usually solve the problem, but this vulnerability is worth considering.

o **Compact Flash.** These are the most common form of storage card. They are a bit thicker than a SmartMedia card. If your camera accepts a Type II Flash Card (thicker than its sibling, the more common Type I), you can also use a SuperDrive card that contains a tiny hard drive with up to a gigabyte (1,000 MB) of capacity.

o **Memory Stick.** Used for Sony cameras, they're about the size of a stick of gum and come in the same range of capacities as the other cards.

Expert How-to: Travel with a Digital Camera

Cyndi says: I go on a long photo-shooting trip every year, and for me, traveling with a digital camera is a vacation in itself. No film, no waiting until I get home to see my shots. With digital, your camera becomes an extension of your eye (Figure 2.3).

Figure 2.3 Cyndi and her camera in action.

What to Take

Digital cameras require a little more planning than their traditional cousins. But once you've collected the bare necessities, we guarantee that you'll never regret inviting one along.

Pre-Flight Packing

Because suitcases get lost, and airlines have a limited liability for lost luggage, put the camera in your carry-on bag. Digital cameras don't use film, so airport x-rays won't harm your digital pix. However, close long-term contact with magnets can cause damage. Don't pack magnetic objects (like compasses) together with your flash cards.

Have a charged battery in the camera. In times of heightened security, someone may ask you to prove that your camera is really a camera by shooting a picture with it.

- **Batteries.** You'll need at least one change of batteries and your battery charger. Sure, you can conserve your battery by turning off the display screen, but the display is a big reason to own a digital camera.

- **Camera case.** It's best if you can use the camera while it's in the case. Some cameras (like Cyndi's Canon PowerShot S30) have a lens-protecting door. If you bought this case (Figure 2.4), guess how long you'd keep putting it back on between shots!

- **Lens cleaner.** This specially formulated liquid cleans delicate glass and plastic without streaking. You must use it with a clean, soft cloth to avoid scratching the lens.

○ **Storage.** You need lots more storage space than the 16 MB card that probably came with your camera, and you can't yet walk into a local drugstore to buy another flash card when the first one fills up. Three possible solutions are:

Figure 2.4 Case closed.

- Use several 64 or 128 MB flash cards. They're modular, sturdy and inexpensive. Downside: They are easy to misplace or damage. Because they don't hold a lot of pictures, you can run out of space unexpectedly if you are shooting at high resolution.

- Use a large-capacity storage card. If your camera accepts Flash II cards, an IBM Microdrive will let you store dozens of pictures. Downside: They're not always as resilient as flash cards, and if something goes wrong, you lose *all* your pictures. However, Cyndi never needed the spare flash card she took on her last trip, because her Microdrive performed like a champ, even on hikes and in the rain.

- Bring your computer, and download as you go. With a portable computer and Internet access, you can download your pictures and email them home. Downside: Portable computers are a burden, and are attractive theft-bait. And in many countries, you'll need a veritable ton of gear—plugs, wires, and cables, yuck—just to plug yours in safely (see details below).

Traveling Abroad

In foreign countries, your battery charger may need some help. Most of North and South America runs on 110 volts. Most of the rest of the world runs on 220 or 240 volts. Plug a 110 device into 220 power and sparks really fly.

If your battery charger doesn't show dual input (100–240V), you'll need a voltage converter to use it. You can buy converters on the Internet and in electronics stores. You'll also need a plug adapter (Figure 2.5). Look for a kit that includes a voltage converter and several adapters.

Figure 2.5 This adapter kit will power you all around the world.

There and Back Again

Some important hints for successful travel pictures:

- Play with your new digital friend before you leave. Know your camera's different modes, and experiment with any complicated functions or techniques.

- If you have multiple flash cards, number them with a sharpie pen before you use them, then use the cards in their numbered order to print your shots chronologically when you return.

- Get a collapsible mini-tripod for indoor lighting, timed shots and panoramas. Latch ones are sturdier but twist lock ones are lighter. They can be small enough to fit into a standard camera bag or even a mid-sized purse.

- Don't use a flash to take pictures of far-away things, like cathedral ceilings. The light won't illuminate your target, and you'll blind people nearby. Plus, you could be violating rules by using the flash at all. Very bright light can speed fading of old paint and fabric.

- If you have a rechargeable battery, take it out of your camera before dinner. Put the spare in the camera and charge overnight. Stick to this easy regimen, and you'll almost never run out of juice.

- If you *must* maximize battery life, use the camera's viewfinder, not the LCD display. All the pictures on your flash card can be damaged if your battery dies in the middle of recording a shot.

- Travel offers once-in-a-lifetime picture opportunities. When you find a good one, shoot a lot, varying angles and zoom. Unlike film, you can always delete the duds during a quiet moment.

- Be polite. Some people, particularly in foreign countries, don't want their pictures taken. If you crave a good close-up of a person you don't know, ask permission first.

- Be careful. If you want a group picture, ask another tourist or your tour guide. Digital cameras are more valuable than film cameras. In some countries, yours could disappear with the "helpful" passer-by.

Set Your Camera Options

Digital cameras include many more options than film cameras do. You can use these features to compensate for tricky lighting or artificial light, to change the framing with the zoom, and to choose the type of file the camera will

create for each shot. In this chapter, we cover the most common features found on digital cameras.

Most cameras offer two methods for changing settings. You can set the most commonly used features, like flash settings, with buttons (Figure 3.1). Most of the settings are accessed using a menu, displayed on the camera's LCD. To learn how to specify the settings on your camera, refer to your documentation.

Some cameras have an option that lets you choose whether to have your camera save your setting changes or return to the defaults when you shut off the camera. Check your camera's documentation.

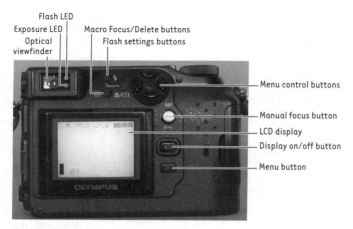

Figure 3.1 Your camera probably lets you set most features with buttons.

Resolution

The camera's resolution setting controls both the file type and the size of the photograph. All cameras can save photos in JPEG format; some also offer the higher resolution TIFF or RAW formats. Within each format setting, you can also choose the resolution or number of pixels that the picture will contain. The more pixels, the higher the resolution and the larger you can display or print the picture without compromising quality.

Choosing the Right Resolution

Before you choose the photo's resolution setting, consider what you plan to do with the picture. If you will print it, you want the highest quality file format (TIFF or RAW). If the picture will be displayed on a Web page or be sent via email, you can use JPEG.

Next, you choose the resolution, which determines the image size of the photo and the amount of information the camera saves for each picture. Resolution settings have names like SHQ (super high quality), also called Fine; HQ (high quality), or Normal; and SQ (standard quality), or Basic.

Why not just take all of your pictures at the highest resolution to get the best quality? For several reasons. First, the higher the resolution, the larger the file size. The larger the file size, the fewer pictures you'll fit on the storage card. For example, on an 8 or 16 MB card, you might only be able to save one or two pictures at the highest resolution. Unless you plan to make a major investment in storage media, that's a pretty big limitation.

Another reason to not use the highest resolution is the law of diminishing returns. If you plan to use the photo on your Web site, the higher resolution is a waste of space, since you'll have to reduce the size of the picture—which will delete the extra pixels.

Remember that you can mix file types and sizes on the same card. So you can use different formats for different pictures just by changing the settings.

Focus

A camera must be set to the right distance for a subject to be in focus. Autofocus will almost always give you the right setting.

Using Autofocus

For most pictures, you can use the autofocus by pointing the camera at the subject and pressing the shutter button. The camera measures the distance to the subject and adjusts the focus accordingly. What could be easier?

Unfortunately, there are a few situations in which autofocus doesn't work correctly without user input. If the subject is not in the center of the frame or there is an excessively bright object near the center, autofocus may not gauge the distance correctly (Figure 3.2).

If you're not sure that the autofocus will know what you are trying to focus on, temporarily move the camera so that the intended subject is centered in the frame, hold the shutter button halfway down, reframe the shot and press the button all the way (Figure 3.3).

Figure 3.2 To keep the glare on the windshield from throwing the autofocus off, first focus on the street and then reframe the shot on the car.

Figure 3.3 Autofocus focused on the closer car, slightly blurring the background (left). Setting the autofocus using the background keeps it in focus, but slightly blurs the car in the foreground (right).

Using macro focus

At normal settings, the closest you can get to a subject and still have it in focus is about 10–12 inches. When you want a super-close shot of something like a flower, you'll need to set the camera to macro focus. At this setting, you can get within a couple of inches and the autofocus will correctly adjust for that distance (Figure 3.4).

Figure 3.4 The camera was about three inches from the flower and was set to macro focus.

Exposure

A camera must be set to let in just the right amount of light in order to get a properly exposed picture. Fortunately, digital cameras are very smart and do this automatically. But there are some situations that call for your input.

What Does Autoexposure Do?

Autoexposure gauges the proper amount of light that the camera requires to get a good shot. Autoexposure usually does the job, but sometimes misreads the correct exposure. Autoexposure, like autofocus, uses the center of the frame to measure the light. So if there is a particularly bright or dark area near the center of the frame, it will throw the exposure off.

To compensate for differing levels of brightness, move the camera so that the area with the correct amount of light is in the center of the frame, then hold the shutter button halfway down. Reframe the shot, then press the button all the way to take the picture (Figure 3.5).

Figure 3.5 The sun behind the trees caused the autoexposure to underexpose this shot (left). Aiming the center of the viewfinder at the ground and holding the shutter button halfway down caused the autoexposure to use the darker area to set the exposure (right).

Zoom

The ability to zoom is one of the handiest features on a camera. Rather than having to move yourself closer or farther from a subject, the zoom allows you to change the apparent distance. So you can make your subject appear to be closer to the camera by zooming in, or you can widen the field to get more in a shot by zooming out (Figure 3.6). Typically, you'll find the zoom control on the top of the camera. Just look through the viewfinder (or LCD display), and push the zoom button to move in or out.

Most digital cameras with both optical and digital zoom are set to use only optical. You can use the camera menu to change this default. The camera will switch to digital

Figure 3.6 Two different views of the same scene, taken from the same spot, using the zoom to change the framing.

zoom when you want to go beyond the optical zoom range. As you zoom, the display will indicate where optical zoom stops and digital zoom begins (Figure 3.7).

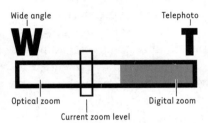

Figure 3.7 The zoom indicator shows you when you have gone past the optical and into digital zoom.

Flash

When there isn't enough light to take good pictures, the camera flash adds enough additional light to give the proper exposure.

Most cameras automatically use the flash when they detect that more light is required, and signal you that the flash is about to fire. There is usually a few seconds' delay while the flash recharges after being used.

Keep in mind that most flashes don't throw their light more than 10 or 15 feet. Anything beyond that range won't get enough light for a proper exposure.

Some cameras offer a flash correction option that lets you set the flash to be brighter or darker. This can be helpful when you need to use the flash, but find it is washing out highlight details.

Reducing red eye

Most cameras offer a red-eye-reduction flash setting. The flash fires twice, once to let the subject's eye adjust to the light and then again a second later to actually take the picture. When you use this feature, make sure your subjects know that this will happen, so they don't move between flashes.

Self Timer/Remote Control

If you'd like to take a picture and be in it at the same time, you can use the self timer. Set up the shot on a tripod or other stationary object, then turn on the self timer. The camera will wait a few seconds after you push the shutter button before actually taking the picture, giving you time to get into the shot (Figure 3.8).

Figure 3.8 Kaity became a photographer by pushing the button on the remote control and taking her own picture.

Expert How-to: Shooting Great Kid Pictures

Most kids are thrilled to be photographed, so they make very willing subjects. But they also are easily distracted and have boundless energy. Keeping them involved for the whole time you're shooting can be a challenge.

Setting the Scene

Although you can get some terrific pictures on the spur of the moment, sometimes you want to exercise some control, particularly for holiday cards or photo presents.

Formal shots

Children in their holiday best are a perfect opportunity for a classic photo-studio formal shot. Choose a time when you're most likely to have the kids' interest and cooperation (Figure 3.9). If you are planning to shoot a family gathering, do it early on. Kids have a knack for getting dirty and wrinkled (not to mention tired and cranky), particularly after the meal begins.

Figure 3.9 These two fine girls are looking pleased to be photographed.

When it's time for the photo shoot itself, take lots of shots for as long as you can keep the child still. The more you shoot, the more likely it is that one shot will be perfect.

Clothing, props, and backgrounds

Pictures of children mark important stages in their growth. So don't miss the opportunity to get pictures in team uniforms or party costumes (Figure 3.10). Although basic headshots are always nice, pictures posed with a first bicycle, a new pet or the Grand Canyon in the background will tell a far more compelling story. Take advantage of these props to help make the picture memorable for both you and the child as time goes by.

Figure 3.10 The traditional Korean costume helps make this first birthday party an excellent occasion to capture.

Planned spontaneity

As with props and backgrounds, setting up the shot around an activity is a great way to capture candid, informal photos. A game of softball or a storytelling session will keep the child involved and relaxed and will make for great photos (Figure 3.11).

Preparing the Camera Settings

Once you've set the scene, it's time to prepare your camera. Remember that time is of the essence. The more you mess with settings, the more likely it is that the child will become bored and cranky.

Figure 3.11 Elizabeth stands in to take her first swing at a pitch.

Shooting outdoors

Shooting outdoors gives you endless possibilities for backgrounds and action shots, and it's pretty easy to get great pictures because the auto-exposure handles the light well. Outdoor shots will look best if you wait until the afternoon, when the light is more diffuse (Figure 3.12). Noonday sunlight is more glaring and tends to wash out colors. If you must shoot in bright sunlight, try to find a spot that is partially shaded.

 Sometimes when you are shooting outdoors in shadow, the darker parts of the picture are too dark. Many cameras have a setting called "Fill Flash" that will give you just a touch of extra light to highlight the darker areas.

Figure 3.12 The warm light and long shadows add a nice touch to this family portrait.

Shooting indoors

Indoor photos usually involve the camera's flash, which fortunately works automatically. If you find that the flash is creating too much light and washing out facial highlights, try moving away from the subject and using the zoom. If your camera has a flash compensation feature, you can adjust the brightness to suit your needs.

Red-eye reduction issues

Before using red-eye reduction, let children know that the camera is going to flash twice, or they might well run off after the first flash. If that doesn't work, turn off red-eye reduction. It isn't worth taking the chance that the child will start to cry because of the bright light. You can easily get rid of red-eye later using your picture-editing software.

Helping Children Be Good Subjects

A little preparation goes a long way when you are shooting pictures of children.

o **Focus first.** Set up your camera and any other aspects of the shots before you get your subject involved in the process.

o **Do test shots.** You can have an adult or older child stand in for your actual subject. Shoot several tests and review them on the camera's display, checking that the exposure and background look good.

o **Distract creatively.** You can often keep children still and relaxed just by talking to them (Figure 3.13). Making funny faces and telling knock-knock jokes also gets them laughing, which makes for wonderful portraits. (This technique works well with adults, too.)

Figure 3.13 Max drills an imaginary hole in the floor while photos are snapped.

- **Get others to help you.** Good child portraits don't have to be one-person affairs; getting help from a coopera- tive and patient grown-up will often allow you to con- centrate on your picture-taking and give you a great shot of the child.

- **Avoid self-timer shots.** Although they can work well with older children and adults, very young children can lose their poise when you rush to join them in a photo.

You are making pictures for the ages, so take pictures of several generations in one picture. A photo of a child with parents and grandparents will be treasured for years to come (Figure 3.14).

Figure 3.14 Three generations of the Nebraska Boslaughs.

Transfer and Store Your Photos

Once you have taken your photographs, you'll want to be able to look at them... again and again, in fact. You can do so immediately right on the camera. But

your images are safer and more useful on your computer, where you can see them with more detail, save them in a variety of formats and make backup copies.

This chapter gets your pictures out of the camera, into your computer, and organized for future use.

Choose Your Images

Using the camera's LCD display, you can look at your photographs right after you take them. Because the screen is so small, you'll only be able to get a general sense of what a shot looks like, enough to determine whether the shot came out (they nearly always do), and to check exposure and framing.

Using the Preview

To view the shots stored on your camera, set the camera to viewing mode. The shots will appear on the camera's display (Figure 4.1). Use the buttons on the camera to move from one shot to the next. If your camera has the option to zoom in on each shot, you can get a better view of the finer points, like focus.

Figure 4.1 In Playback mode, the camera becomes the viewer that enables you to see the shots inside.

As you view an unwanted shot, press the Delete button (Figure 4.2), which sometimes has a wastebasket icon. The camera will ask if you really want to delete the shot. Press OK to confirm.

Figure 4.2 The Flash settings button serves as the Delete button in Playback mode.

As with computers, once you have deleted a file, it is REALLY gone. So if you are not sure, err on the side of caution and keep the shot until you can review it on your computer. You can always delete it later.

*Some cameras have functions to process shots while you are reviewing them. You can change a shot to black & white or sepia tone, or add filter effects like starbursts. We **strongly** recommend against using these features. Image editing software will do this more effectively without changing the original shot.*

Connect to Your Computer

Most new cameras connect directly to your computer via USB port and cable. You just run the software that came with your camera after you make the connection. If your camera isn't USB ready, or if you have an old computer without a USB port, you should get a card reader instead.

If your computer does not have a USB port, you can generally add one using a USB PCI card (for desktop computers) or PC card (for laptops). These cards are under $40 and fairly easy to install.

To connect your camera to your computer, first check the camera's documentation to see if you must install software first. If so, follow the instructions provided.

Depending on your camera and its software, you'll either be able to see the camera as if it were a disk, like a floppy, or you'll have to use a program provided to transfer your photos.

- **Connecting to a PC.** When you connect your camera directly to a Windows computer, you'll need to run the software that came with the camera to view and transfer shots. After you plug in the camera, just start up the software and follow the instructions.

  When connecting to a card reader, follow the manual's instructions on how to install the drivers, then plug in the reader and restart the computer, Insert a flash card into the reader and double-click My Computer to show the reader listed as a drive (Figure 4.3).

Figure 4.3 The card reader—Removable Disk [H:]—is displayed in My Computer as it were another disk drive.

- **Connecting to a Mac.** When you plug a USB-equipped camera or card reader into your Macintosh version 8.5 or higher, it will appear on your desktop as a disk drive icon (Figure 4.4). You can double-click on the icon and copy your shots by dragging them to a folder on your hard drive.

 If you are connecting the camera through a USB port, you can usually just plug the camera in, even with the computer running. If you are connecting with a serial port, check your manual to see if you need to shut the computer off before connecting the camera. You usually do.

Important: Always make sure that the camera is turned off before you remove the storage card.

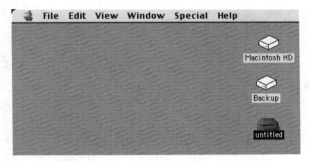

Figure 4.4 The drive icon called Untitled is the card in the reader.

Transfer Your Photos

Some storage cards are locked when you use them on your computer, so you can copy *from* them but not *to* them. If your card is not locked, you can forget to copy a photo from the card before tinkering with it. In a word, *don't*. It's very important that you work on a copy of the picture, and leave the original intact. Also, saving anything to the card while it is in the computer can corrupt the card and require you to reformat it in the camera, which will wipe out any pictures still on the card.

Transferring from Flash Card to Computer

Before transferring files to your computer, create a new folder to store them. In Windows, right-click and choose New Folder. Right-click on the new folder and choose Rename. Give it a descriptive name. On a Macintosh, choose File > New Folder. This will create an icon called "Untitled Folder." Click on the folder name and rename it appropriately.

With your storage card in the reader, the card appears and can be used just like a drive. Double-click to open it, double-click folders inside to open them until you see files with suffixes like .jpg or .tif, then copy these files to your hard drive. The easiest way to transfer the files to your computer is to choose Select All from the Edit menu and then use the mouse to drag the selected files to your new folder (Figure 4.5).

Some programs, like Photoshop Elements, have an Acquire feature that will copy the files from the card onto your hard drive.

 Windows users: After you select the files on the card, you can right-click on any of the files and choose Copy. Then, go to the folder on the other drive, right-click again and choose Paste.

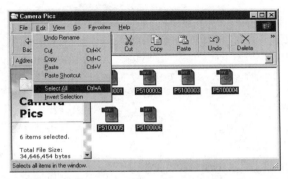

Figure 4.5 Select All is the fastest way to select every file in a folder.

Erasing your flash card

Once you have transferred your shots from the card (and double-checked to make sure they were copied OK), you can erase them from the card.

In Windows, select the files, right-click the mouse and choose Delete. The files are gone and your card is back to maximum capacity. On a Macintosh, select the files, drag them to the Trash and choose Special > Empty Trash. Drag the card's image to the Trash to eject it.

Never delete the folders that appear on the card, just the photo files. If the folders get deleted, you will have to reformat the card in the camera.

Viewing your transferred photos

Once you have transferred your photos to the computer, you'll want to review them to see which to keep, which to send to friends, and of course, which duds to dump. Your editing software provides a convenient way to see all of the shots in a particular folder. They will appear as small "thumbnails" that you can double-click to view and edit in full size (Figure 4.6).

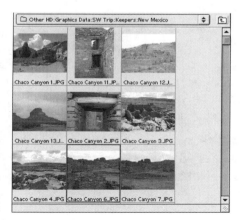

Figure 4.6 The File Browser shows all of the pictures in a folder.

Save and Organize Photos

The more you use your camera, the more shots you are going to have to keep track of. It is important to set up some kind of system for organizing your work. You can use the same techniques to organize digital photos as you do to organize any other kind of computer data.

Renaming Transferred Photos

When the camera takes a shot, it gives it a cryptic name like P10001.jpg. This doesn't tell you much about what's in the shot. So it's best to rename images as soon as you transfer them to the computer.

The easiest method for renaming is to use your image editor to open each shot, then choose File > Save As to give it a new name.

Even if your shots are in JPG format, it is best to save them as TIFF files to retain the highest resolution. (See *What are File Types?* below for more on file formats.)

When you have finished renaming all the shots in a folder, you can get rid of the ones with the cryptic names, since they have been replaced with copies.

Saving Your Original Shots

You can save the same shot in different ways depending on what you want to do with it. You might have a medium-quality version to post on your Web page and a lower quality (and therefore smaller) version to send via email. Each version should have a different name. Keep the original unchanged, so if you use it for something in the future, like making a print, you'll have the original at the highest resolution.

Keeping originals also provides you with a safety net if you make changes to a shot in your editing software and the results aren't exactly what you were looking for.

 One of the best ways to preserve your original shots is to burn them onto a CD. See Chapter 1 for more details.

Expert How-to: What are File Types (and Why Should I Care)?

In Chapter 3, we told you that you could set your camera to different resolutions for different quality, and that many cameras can shoot in different file types: JPEG, TIFF, or RAW. You probably skipped over this second part, but it can be very important. Each file type has a unique format in which it saves image information. The format you shoot, edit and save in can make a big difference in the quality of a printed picture.

Like film types, file types have been designed to do some things very well, at the expense of other things. It's up to you to choose the right one for your needs.

o **JPEG file type.** Every digital camera uses this file type as its default. In fact, if your camera documentation doesn't tell you how to change file format, it means you can only shoot in JPEG.

The JPEG formula analyzes the raw image, and dumps some color data to make very small image files. At the highest quality setting, the JPEG format throws out only a little data but makes larger files; with the lowest setting, it throws out a lot, but makes very small files.

Quality is often confused with resolution, but they measure different things. *Resolution* is measured by the number of pixels in the picture. *Quality* is how much color information JPEG compression maintains. The lower the quality, the more changes are made to your image.

 If you want an ultra-high-quality print, begin by shooting in TIFF or RAW format. If you can only shoot in JPEG, choose your camera's Superhigh Quality setting (Figure 4.7).

Figure 4.7 Here's an example of the choices you get in one camera. Besides TIFF, the options are Superhigh Quality, High Quality and Standard Quality. You'll find these settings in your camera's menu.

○ **TIFF file type.** Some digital cameras give you the option of saving files in TIFF format rather than JPEG. If you want a picture with all its original data intact, TIFF is a good choice, because it doesn't throw away any image data. Serious photographers use TIFF to maintain as much information for printing as they can.

○ **RAW file type.** Cameras that don't offer a TIFF option sometimes offer RAW instead. RAW is exactly what it sounds like: unaltered, pristine image data. It's what the camera actually sees when it takes your picture. Like TIFFs, RAW files are favorites of serious photographers, and are usually only available on more expensive camera models.

File types compared

The best thing about JPEGs is that even the highest quality ones have very small file sizes, so you'll fit more of them on your storage card. But JPEG images are meant to be used at exactly the same size and resolution at which they were created. If you enlarge, edit or otherwise change a JPEG on the computer, you'll notice errors you couldn't see before.

The big problem with TIFFs is...they're big. Shoot the same picture as a high-quality JPEG and a TIFF, and you'll see the difference in file size immediately (Figure 4.8). As a result, you'll fit very few pictures on a flash card. Even worse, a TIFF on a 3-megapixel camera can easily take 20 seconds for the camera to process—not exactly suitable for action shots, or even children's birthday parties.

Is the quality difference worth the megabytes? Only if you're going to wallpaper your room with pictures. At snapshot size, you really can't tell the difference between a good JPEG and a TIFF. For enlargements, you can always change your JPEG to a TIFF on the computer to help maintain quality.

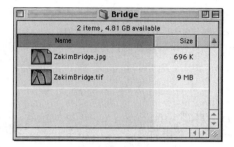

Figure 4.8 A reasonably sized JPEG file is much bigger once it's turned into a TIFF.

If you do expect to print large photos, spend the extra money for a camera that creates RAW images. RAW files are only a little larger than a high-quality JPEG, and are tiny compared to a TIFF of the same image. Besides, you *can* turn them into a TIFF—the ideal file type for editing—on the computer.

Changing file types

There are several good reasons to change your file format after you load your pictures into your computer. The most important is that JPEG is a *bad* format for image editing. Every time you resave as JPEG, the quality of the image gets worse, no matter what "quality" setting you choose for the file.

Very important: You should change to TIFF before you begin editing, resizing or even rotating a picture. You should change to JPEG just before you send the file to print, or upload it to an online service or a Web page.

Changing to a TIFF

To change from JPEG to TIFF, just open the file, choose File > Save As, and choose TIFF from the Format menu in the Save As dialog box (Figure 4.9).

There are no special settings to worry about when you save a file as a TIFF. Just accept the defaults that appear in dialog boxes, then make any image changes you'd like. Remember not to change back to JPEG until you're done editing.

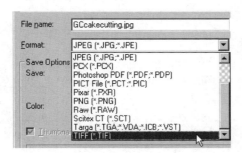

Figure 4.9 If your editing program supports more than one file format, there'll be a drop-down menu for file types in the Save As dialog box.

Changing back to JPEG

Changing back to JPEG from TIFF is not quite as straight-forward, because you have to select a quality setting. Software programs give you more quality options than cameras do, but the scale they use varies from program to program. For example, Adobe software uses a quality scale from 0 to 12, with 12 being the highest quality and 0 the lowest. Many other applications use a scale from 1 to 99 or 100. The confusing part is that on this scale, 100 is the lowest quality, and 1 is the best (Figure 4.10). These scales don't correspond to one other—or to camera settings—in any way, except by chance.

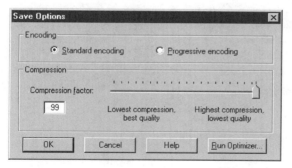

Figure 4.10 This application measures the highest quality as 1, and the lowest as 99.

The quality you choose depends on what you want to do with the file. To get a decent 4″ × 6″ full-color print on photo paper, your quality level should range from 10–12 in Adobe programs and from 1–20 in programs where the highest quality is 1. By comparison, you can often go as low as 3 in an Adobe program for images that you'll post on a Web page. Experiment to find what looks best to your eye (Figure 4.11).

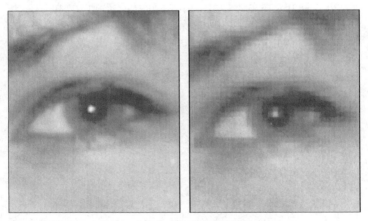

Figure 4.11 As you can see, the images degrade more as you lower the quality setting. But remember, these pictures have been printed. Onscreen, even a fairly low-quality image can still be an acceptable picture.

Improve Your Pictures

Digital cameras make it easier to take great photos, because their quality is consistent and you can see your results instantaneously. But even a good photo can often use a little help to become a great one. When your picture is too dark or your subjects look like red-eyed werewolves, you need photo-editing software to save the day.

This chapter introduces you to different types of photo editing software and the tools that will help you get the most out of the editing experience.

Editing Software

There are three types of software for editing your pictures:

o **Photo organizing software.** These types of programs emphasize cataloging functions, like grouping pictures into albums. You can usually rotate and crop images, and also use a one-step quick fix for standard photo problems. Good examples are Jasc After Shot for Windows and iPhoto or iView Media Pro for Macintosh. Also, most Web-based services offer this type of software online.

○ **Photo editing software.** Besides cropping and resizing, programs of this type let you fix red eye, adjust brightness and contrast, and help you improve pictures with color and sharpness problems. Sometimes they also offer cataloging options and recipes for projects. Examples include Microsoft Picture It for Windows, Graphic-Converter for Macintosh, and Adobe Photoshop Elements for both.

○ **Image editing software.** Designed for both picture editing and creating, image editing software adds painting tools, filters and ways to combine pictures creatively. They often have sophisticated ways to improve photos, but may lack a red-eye tool. They almost never have cataloging options or other project-based features. Some good ones are Jasc Paint Shop Pro for Windows, and MicroFrontier ColorIt! for Macintosh.

Base the type of software you choose on what you expect to do with the pictures. Why buy features you won't use? If you have artistic talent or some time to spare, you might find image editing software exciting. To just fix red eye and recenter a picture, look for an image cataloger with red eye and cropping options. If you're not sure, we recommend the middle ground. Photo editing software is a great way to take control of your pictures while getting your feet wet on the creative side.

Editing Tools

Every editing program has a slightly different approach, arranges its tools somewhat differently and uses different icons. The following tools are those common to most programs.

Selection tools

Selection tools are key to good editing, because you need a way to tell your program what you'd like to change. You need at least two selection tools for photo editing: the marquee and the magic wand. The marquee selects geometric areas: squares, rectangles, circles and ovals (Figure 5.1). You click in one corner of the area you want to select, and the selected area grows as you drag the mouse.

Figure 5.1 In some programs the marquee is one tool with variations for different types of geometric shapes. Other programs give you different marquees for squares and circles.

The magic wand selects areas of similar color. You click on the image, and the computer finds adjacent areas that are approximately the same hue. This is a good tool for selecting an object with its shadows and bright spots (Figure 5.2).

In most programs, you can add to an existing selection by holding down the Shift key while you click a different area.

Figure 5.2 The magic wand is good for large areas of continuous tone, like the sky, that have variations of the same basic color.

Cropping tool

Cropping tools allow you to select a rectangular area on the screen and cut away anything that isn't inside that selected area. A cropping tool should give you two ways to crop: by choosing a specific dimension (like 4″ × 6″ for a standard print) or by drawing a rectangle to describe the area you want, even if that area isn't a standard size (Figure 5.3).

Figure 5.3 Photoshop Elements allows you to easily adjust the position of the crop outline, as well as its length and width.

Red-eye reduction tool

Although many digital cameras have a red-eye reduction function (see Chapter 3), it's not foolproof. You'll frequently get red eye in your photos even if you use it. Because this problem is so prevalent, all photo editing software offers some type of red-eye reduction tool (Figure 5.4).

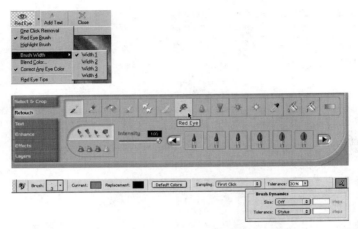

Figure 5.4 Three different applications' version of the red-eye reduction tool. Jasc After Shot has only four brush sizes, and works best with closeups (top). PhotoExpression's icons and sliders easily handle a variety of eye sizes (middle). Photoshop Elements offers a good balance of simplicity and power (bottom).

Red-eye reduction tools work by recognizing the specific shade and intensity of red that reflects back from the pupil, removing the red color, then darkening the area. Red eye tools that are applied with a brush are better than those that are applied by drawing a box around the eye. Tools that select this way are less precise; they often spill into portions of the eye that aren't red (Figure 5.5).

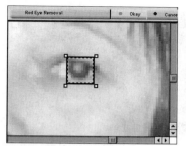 

Figure 5.5 Ofoto's red-eye reduction is applied by drawing a box around the eye area. In this image, which was shot at low resolution, using the red-eye reduction tool distorts the eye. It was impossible to get the box small enough to exactly select the red area.

Contrast and brightness tool

You'll frequently see a slider tool called Brightness/Contrast. These two changes are combined because they are very similar functions. The computer determines how light or dark a pixel is on a scale of 0 (black) to 255 (white). Adding numbers increases brightness, subtracting decreases it. Be cautious when increasing brightness; if you add too much, all the colors will wash out. Contrast works by allowing you to make pixels that are already dark even darker, and light pixels even lighter (Figure 5.6).

Figure 5.6 We've greatly increased the image contrast on the left and the brightness on the right.

Hue tool

On the computer, the rainbow of visible color is created using the light of three primary colors, or *hues*: red, green and blue. Tools that shift hue may be called Color Cast, Color Balance, Color Correction, or Hue/Saturation. They are usually made up of several sliders that let you change the way your picture's color range is organized (Figure 5.7).

If you eliminate one color of the three completely, the image looks psychedelic. But if you increase or decrease one color

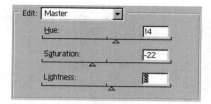

Figure 5.7 The hue slider allows you to move all the colors in a picture toward blue (left), green (right) or red (middle). The Saturation slider adds or decreases color. The Lightness slider brightens or darkens.

just a little, you can repair the colors in a picture, like one that was shot indoors, and looks too red or blue because of artificial light.

Sharpen tool

Many images can benefit from a little bit of definition. The Sharpen tool provides that extra improvement.

It's easy to over-apply sharpening; the result will look faked or oddly textured (Figure 5.8). But applied sparingly, Sharpen will punch up an image nicely.

Sharpen doesn't help an out-of-focus picture. It sees every place where there is a difference in the color of adjoining pixels as an edge, creating patterns and distorting rather than clarifying.

Figure 5.8 This image is over-sharpened. In the sharpened area on the left, the child's face is pebbled, and her hair clip has a white edge around it.

Quick Fix tool

Many programs offer a quick fix option, which looks at a photo and makes standard adjustments in color, brightness and contrast. This option tends to work pretty well if the problem with the image isn't extreme. It tends to work badly if the photo was shot at night without a flash, or if you have already made edits before using the quick fix (Figure 5.9).

Figure 5.9 The original picture, taken in a dark restaurant, was so dark that you could barely see the image. The quick fix setting (left) is a great improvement, but is not as good as adjusting color, brightness, contrast, saturation and sharpening by eye (right).

Expert How-to: Using Editing Software

Digital camera settings allow you to correct for all sorts of difficult shooting situations, but you have to remember to change those settings before you shoot. In real life, pictures happen suddenly, and sometimes photographers forget the basics in the excitement of a terrific event. The inevitable result is photos that, if shot with film, would end up in the circular file. But a digital camera gives you a second chance. Here are some hints for applying editing software to some of those imperfect moments.

Fixing brightness and contrast

The most common problem is shots that are too dark or light. Before you try to correct for brightness, temporarily change your image from color to grayscale. (Some editing software has a button to do this quickly. If yours doesn't, look for a menu called Mode and select from the list.) Does the picture still look too bright or dark? If so, undo the change and continue editing. But your picture may look fine in grayscale. If so, changing the image brightness will simply make your image worse.

When you use the Brightness/Contrast sliders, watch your image very carefully; a little change can have big consequences. Move the brightness slider two or three units to the left or right, depending on your problem. When adding brightness, watch the important, brightest places on the image as you do this. When they start to lose detail, you've gone too far (Figure 5.10). When darkening an image, you should be watching detail in the shadows.

It's the rare picture that can be adjusted without moving the contrast slider, too. If you have made the picture much brighter, you will probably have to decrease the contrast a little, or else both bright and dark areas will lose more detail.

In any event, don't move these sliders more than 10 units in either direction for a normal picture. Anything more will either wash out the picture or make it look like it was shot in a cave.

Figure 5.10 Look at the cake on the left. All the detail in the frosting is disappearing as the brightness increases. If the bright places don't matter so much, you might just keep going. But in this case, the cake cutting is the major action in the photo.

Correcting color shifts

If you are shooting in certain lighting, like indoors with artificial light, you can wind up with odd-looking results: A shot may wind up looking too red or too green. A color shift like this can ruin an otherwise well-composed and photographed image.

Digital cameras have a marvelous feature called *white balance* that will correct this kind of problem before it happens. By setting the camera to correct for different types of light as you shoot, you can get a good looking photograph without having to do extensive color correction in your image editing software. But the camera's setting doesn't always gauge the lighting situation perfectly.

To fix a color problem in an image, move the Hue slider a little bit away from the center (toward the green shades if the picture was shot in incandescent light, toward the red shades if under fluorescent light).

Next, you need to lower the saturation slightly, to neutralize the shift toward red or green. Every program's sliders are calibrated a little differently, but you'll probably find acceptable results between –5 and –15 on the Saturation slider. If your Hue/Saturation tool also has a Brightness slider, add or subtract a little brightness as well (Figure 5.11).

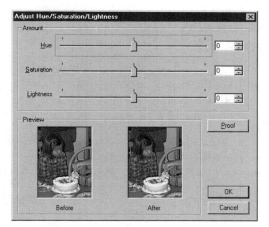

Figure 5.11 The Hue/Saturation tool can improve your color shift problem. You can shift the hue, make everything less vibrant, or you can lighten the colors to make the color shift less noticeable.

Creative Changes

Tone and color changes are really just the beginning of what you can do with your photos on the computer. With an image editing program, you can delete unwanted objects, retouch pictures to make people look better, and merge two or more different photos seamlessly. You can add pictures to family newsletters, or add text to turn your photo into a greeting card. We cover all of these possibilities and more, in *The Little Digital Camera Book*.

Save, and Save Again

If there is any one critical piece of advice about image editing, this is it: **Never** edit the original file. Editing an original file is like shredding a film negative, and just as permanent.

Before you even open a file in an editing program, make a duplicate of it. (On the Mac, that's Command-D, on the PC, use Ctrl-C then Ctrl-V.) The duplicate will have the word copy in its filename. Edit only the copy. If you want to start again from scratch, make a second duplicate, so you'll never have to touch the original.

Making Multiple Image Corrections

Order is important for image editing. Follow this step-by-step cheat sheet to do your edits in the right order for optimum quality and safety.

1. Change the photos you want to edit from JPEG files into TIFF files so you won't lose image quality.

2. Make red eye reductions.

3. Adjust color problems.

4. Adjust brightness and contrast problems.

5. Save before changing resolution, cropping or scaling.

6. Change resolution or image size.

7. If it needs it, sharpen the image.

8. Save as a TIFF for the last time.

9. Save as a JPEG at the correct quality setting.

Print Your Images

We love the instant gratification of seeing pictures onscreen, but there's still nothing like having a color print. Fortunately, it's just as easy to make prints from your digital images as from traditional film. Easier, actually, since you can do it all without leaving home.

Why Print at Home?

Admittedly, professional services are a real time- and hassle-saver. Besides, unless you were a serious photo hobbyist (or professional), you never processed your pictures by yourself with a regular camera. Why bother with it now?

o Because you can. Setting up a darkroom to process film is messy and expensive. But setting up for digital printing merely requires plugging one USB cable into your computer and installing a printer driver.

o Because you want it now. At home, you shoot, you print. With a photo service, you shoot, you upload (or drop off), then you wait.

- Because it's a sure way to get your whole print. Digital cameras take pictures at a different proportion than photo services print them. So if you shoot a 4.5 × 6-inch snapshot, for example, when you get that picture back from a professional developer, they'll have run it through a cookie cutter to make it 4 × 6 inches, slicing off some of your picture in the process.

- Because photo services can change your print. Some services apply a quick fix to improve your photos (Figure 6.1). If you print the picture yourself, you can adjust the photo—or not—to suit your eye.

Figure 6.1 The original digital photo was shot at dusk (left). The 4″ × 6″ print has been cropped and brightened to look like late afternoon (right).

Inkjet Printers and Cartridges

To print at home, you need a photo-quality color printer. Inkjet printers are your best choice if you want to use one printer for both photos and text.

One of the big misconceptions about inkjet printers is that if you purchase a printer that promises photo quality, you've got the right printer for photos. In fact, there are two different types of color inkjet printers: general purpose and photo. Your choice can make all the difference in the quality and durability of your photo prints.

General-purpose printers are used for a variety of home and business purposes, including photo printing. Photo printers use special inks and paper that are optimized for photographic images. Although you can frequently use the same paper in both types, and a photo printed on both can look almost the same, they are really very different products. General-purpose inkjets, like Epson's Stylus series, are cheap and fast. Because they're seen as small-business printers, they're optimized for text rather

than images, and they print reasonably well on plain laser paper.

Photo printers not only will give you better quality pictures, but those pictures will last longer. Many photo printers use special inks and papers to make them more resistant to moisture and fading. Those special inks make photo printers a little more expensive to own and run. And because a photo print needs lots of ink, some photo printers run through cartridges a little faster than all-purpose printers.

Buying Considerations

You can buy a general purpose inkjet printer for under $100. A basic photo inkjet will cost closer to $150. In most cases, the technology of a $150 photo printer won't be much different than one that costs $500. The differences? More expensive printers usually process more information, which tends to make them slower. They're also larger, enabling you to print your own blowups. And they often have larger-capacity inkjet cartridges.

Make sure that the printer you choose has the software to make it work with your computer. The best printer is of little value if you can't use it. For example, many older inkjet printers that you might find on eBay won't work with newer software and operating systems.

Despite these limitations, you should unquestionably buy a photo printer if most of your printing will be for digital photos. You can still print lower-quality prints for other purposes.

 If you've already bought a general-purpose printer, check out third-party makers of inks and paper. Some enterprising companies are making waterproof paper and inks for non–photo printers.

Types of Cartridges

Because you'll be burning through cartridges furiously, you'll want to look at the type of cartridge your printer uses. Manufacturers make a printer with two cartridges: one for black and one for the other colors, or they can create individual cartridges for each color.

It's more convenient—and cost-effective—for the manufacturer to make only two cartridges. Fewer cartridges are more convenient for you, the consumer, as well. You don't have to pay attention to which ink color is going bad, and you don't have to constantly keep an inventory of how many cartridges of each color you have. On the other hand, this multicolor concept wastes ink, because you're unlikely to use all the colors equally fast.

Making Your Inkjet Photos Last Forever

People used to complain bitterly about how quickly digital prints faded compared with traditional photos. Some prints still do. But if you print with a newer-model photo printer and follow some basic guidelines, your prints can last as long as professional ones.

- Use the right paper and inks. Read your printer documentation's paper and ink recommendations carefully.

- Give prints time to dry. Photo prints need a little time to "set." Don't stack your prints immediately after you print them.

- Keep prints out of direct sunlight. Light is the enemy of all photo prints, whether traditional or digital.

- Frame your prints properly if you want to display them. A print under glass will last considerably longer than one left in the open air.

- Watch out for "magnetic" photo albums. The stuff that makes the plastic stick to the page can react with your inkjet prints, with horrid results.

- Stay away from heat and moisture. The combination will make prints stick together, bleed color, and otherwise ruin some perfect photo moments.

You'll end up throwing out cartridges that still have plenty of ink because a single color has run dry. And because multicolor cartridges also tend to contain very little ink per color well, you'll be changing (and discarding) cartridges more frequently—an environmental concern.

On the other hand, the more colors you print with, the better. Printers that use six colors will produce pictures that are more realistic and professional than those that use four. They are a little more expensive to buy and run, but can be well worth the difference in quality.

Paper Types

You need to consider two things when buying paper: weight and finish. Photo paper needs to be thicker than standard office or inkjet paper, because when you print a photo, you cover the entire sheet with ink, so you need a paper that won't bend and buckle like a wet newspaper.

The other important consideration is the paper finish. Like house paint, paper finishes range from matte, to satin, to high gloss. Your choice is a matter of taste, of course, but some finishes lend themselves better to different types of usage. If you plan to display a photo in bright light, you should probably steer away from a high-gloss paper, because people looking at it will see the reflections better than they will the photo. Of course, before you buy a paper, check to see that it's one your printer manufacturer recommends. We cover printers and papers in more detail in *The Little Digital Camera Book*.

Having Professionals Do It

We like to print some photos ourselves, but when you've got 60 shots to print, sitting in front of a computer for a few hours is going to feel like a chore. Fortunately, there are lots of companies practically jumping up and down for the opportunity to do all that printing for you.

Online Photo Printing Services

To use a service, you'll need an account, but setting one up is easy. In most cases, all you need to do is supply an email address, a password, and your full name and address (for mailing your prints back to you).

Just as it's a little more expensive to purchase the basics for a digital camera, it's a little more expensive to get professional prints from them as well. The lowest prices for digital prints can be twice what you pay for film developing. You'll pay extra for each double print (though prices will drop as volume rises), and for shipping.

To avoid being disappointed by poor print quality, check the resolution of your images before you upload them.

You'll have to cultivate some patience in return for convenience. You won't get your prints the same day or even overnight. In fact, depending on your choice of service, you could wait from three days to a week before the prints arrive.

Quality varies, but ranges from acceptable to really good. We particularly like Snapfish (www.snapfish.com) and PhotoAccess (www.photoaccess.com). Most services provide 4″ × 6″ prints as their standard snapshot, in addition to wallet prints (nice and cheap) and larger sizes (rather expensive). Surprisingly few make 3″ × 5″ prints. That's a problem if you have a low resolution camera, or want to fit your pictures into a standard photo album. One of those that does is PhotoAccess, which also provides very fast shipping to most destinations.

Printing very high resolution shots can cause problems for some online services. Transfers can fail if they're interrupted in the middle of uploading, and the pictures grab lots of online space. In fact, some services enforce a maximum size for each picture, so read the fine print of the service's upload policy before you begin.

Share Your Photos

Is there anyone who doesn't have photos tucked away in boxes, drawers, and closets? You keep them because they're part of your history, and because you imagine that someday you'll trot them out for friends and family. Sharing your memories gets a lot easier with digital photos. Not only can you show your pictures immediately, but your pictures are available at any time, day or night, to anyone you want to share them with. In this chapter, we examine the growing number of options digital camera owners have for their images.

Emailing Your Images

The most immediate way of sharing photos computer-to-computer is to email them. They stay digital, and one electronic photo spawns dozens of copies with no effort on your part. All recent versions of email software have simple ways to attach pictures to email. Your recipient can view any JPEG file in a browser window, without additional software.

Preparing a File for Emailing

Unless you are sending lots of photos at the same time, the best type of picture file to send is JPEG. As we discussed earlier, JPEGs can be saved at different quality levels. The lower the quality, the smaller the file. But pictures can have very low quality and resolution and still look terrific onscreen.

You can't go wrong with most pictures if you use a resolution of 72 dpi, a quality setting of 4, and a maximum on-screen picture size of 740 by 450 pixels (Figure 7.1).

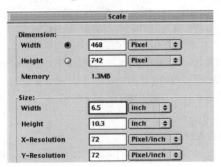

Figure 7.1 These settings are just about where you want them to be for an emailed image.

Why Do You Need Compression?

JPEGs are already compressed files, and they're a universally accepted format. If you've prepared your pictures properly, they're the best way to send your photos. But if you plan to send dozens of JPEGs at a time, or JPEGs at a high quality for printing, you may need to gather them into folders. Since email programs can't handle folders as attachments, you'll need to compress the folder first. Additional compression is also particularly useful if you or one of your JPEG recipients uses a dial-up modem, which has a low file transfer speed.

Compressing Files

When you want to compress your files, first put them all in one folder on your desktop, then run the compression software on the whole folder.

In Windows, you'll need software that creates ZIP files. The best-known low-priced programs to do this are:

- WinZip (www.winzip.com/)(comes installed on some computers as a trial application)
- PKZIP (www.pkware.com/)

On a Macintosh, to make SIT files, you'll need:

- StuffIt Deluxe; or
- StuffIt Lite (www.stuffit.com/)

When sending compressed files between Mac and Windows, you need to make sure recipients can open and view their pictures. The company that makes StuffIt, Aladdin Systems (www.aladdinsys.com), includes a program called DropZip in StuffIt Lite that lets Mac users make ZIP files.

In any case, if the recipient has the right software installed, the email software should prompt the decompression part of the software to go to work when the email and attachment arrive at their destination.

Receiving Compressed Mac Files on a PC

Netscape's Messenger and Microsoft's Outlook Express automatically decompress all compressed files you receive. Unfortunately, if you are a Windows user receiving a compressed SIT file from a Mac user, the email program will decompress the files the wrong way, stripping away elements that these files need to be read properly again on any platform.

If you are a Windows user with lots of Macintosh friends (or one really good Mac friend), we recommend that you download the free version of Stuffit Expander for Windows from Aladdin Systems, which will decompress both SIT and ZIP files. That way, you'll always be able to read compressed files sent to you by Macintosh users.

Attaching an Image to Email

When an email program sends attachments, it encodes (translates) them into a special format to send them successfully over the Internet. Unfortunately, not all email systems and computer platforms use the same method of encoding. When you send a file in one encoding scheme to an email program using a different scheme, the files become corrupted and won't open, or won't open properly.

Most current email software uses a type of encoding called MIME (Multipurpose Internet Mail Extensions) as its default. If your email doesn't, you should be able to change the setting to this encoding method. If you're sending from a Macintosh email program to a Windows user, it's particularly important to locate this setting. See your program's Help files for details.

Sending and receiving attachments in AOL

Email is not AOL's strong suit. In versions prior to 7.0, you can't send embedded images (images inserted within the body of the email message), except to other AOL users. And if someone from outside AOL sends you attachments without compressing them, they will become garbled and impossible to view. AOL users wanting to send and receive photos outside AOL should upgrade to version 7.0, or at least should compress everything as an attachment.

Online Photo Services

Online photo services are in the business of photo sharing. If they don't make it easy for you to use them, they
won't be around for very long. There's no reason to settle
for a service that doesn't have all the options that you like.
By all means, try out more than one while you're still exper-
imenting with image sharing. You might find that one service is particularly good for special gift ideas like making
T-shirts and greeting cards (Figure 7.2), but costs more than
you'd like for prints.

Figure 7.2 PhotoAccess offers great options for all things photo.
Besides the usual T-shirts and caps, they'll apply your image to
everything from a puzzle to the paper you wrap the gift in.

Using Photo Service Pages

Two of the most popular options offered by online photo services are customer Web pages and photo albums. The biggest difference between the two is that Web pages are open to the entire world. With photo albums, only those people that you want to see them can do so. Creating an album or Web page is easy: If you know how to upload a file, you can display your images online.

Shutterfly's options are typical of most services. First you select an album to share, next you create a list of your recipients' email addresses, and then you create an email invitation to view your photos at the service's site (Figure 7.3). You set the level of access for your mailing list: everyone is allowed to view the pictures and order copies, or you could require them to sign in to Shutterfly.

 Be sure to warn your friends if you have uploaded low-resolution pictures for display only. If they order prints of low-resolution files, they'll be very unhappy with the poor quality of the prints.

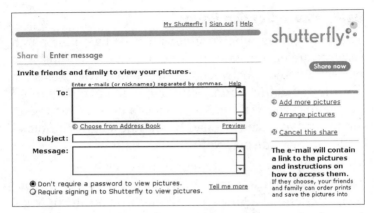

Figure 7.3 Shutterfly lets you invite friends to view your photos online.

Selecting an Online Service

Although you can use more than one service for different things, in practice most people stick with one or two favorites. You can spend a significant amount of time uploading pictures to a site, and if you use more than one site or change sites after you've uploaded, most of the time you'll have to upload all over again. So when it comes to online services, it pays to read the fine print. Some things to consider when choosing your online service:

○ Are the photos secure? Sometimes we share photos with friends that we might not want everyone else in the world to see. Every reputable service should have a prominently posted security policy.

○ Is the service financially stable? If the service is slow to respond to your questions or frequently threatens changes in pricing or policy, you should start looking for a new service.

○ Is the service free? Some services are only free for a trial period; after that they charge a monthly fee.

○ Does the service have a maximum storage limit? If so, what is it? Most photo services limit the amount of space you can use to store your pictures. Three exceptions are Ofoto, Shutterfly, and PhotoAccess. But if you don't post a lot of pictures or you only upload pictures at low resolution, that limited space may be unlimited for your purposes.

○ Will the service erase the files eventually? Some services don't limit your amount of space, but do limit how long you can have it there. FotoTime, for example, gives you 30 days to decide whether to use their service. If you don't subscribe by the end of that period, they delete the images in your storage space.

Index